Inside the Deep

Brittney Zapata

BookLeaf
Publishing

India | USA | UK

Presentation by *BookLeaf Publishing*

Web: www.bookleafpub.com

E-mail: info@bookleafpub.com

ISBN: 9789358311358

First edition 2023

To my family and friends I love you

ACKNOWLEDGEMENT

I want to thank my mom, two best friends, and sister in law for showing me that can love exist.

Run

I just want to run

Run from the fears
that clings on the tears

Run from the past
that took me to fast

Run from the chain
that clings to the pain

Run from the voices
that gives many choices

I just want to run...from me

Giving & Taking

I hear you and agree with you
You don't hear me you disagree with me

I cave and give you what you want
You question, and I must reason

I explain over and over, time after time
Yet you still won't fix it or even try

I cry in the dark, night after night
You sleep like rock, with no thought in mind

I'm losing you but losing me
Please don't let this be...

One Day

If you had one day with me..

Would you hold my hand along the ocean shore
Or snuggle close as the thunder starts to roar
We would laugh and cry
as we look up at the sky

If you had hours with me...

Would you drive with me to nowhere
Music loud, windows down feeling the air
as we cruise with no care

If you had minutes with me...

Would you sing one song
It doesn't have to be long
I'll even sing along

If you had a seconds with me

Would you tell you me you love me?

This is me

The hand I had, is now a ghost I once felt
My bet is over, the cards are dealt
A new pain rises, deep inside my mind
The iron is strong, I'm being confined

The warmth I feel, within my soul
Is now cold and bitter, I'm losing control
It's dark and empty deep inside
I scream and beg, for a place to hide

I gaze in the mirror, only to see me
Really, could it be?
The eyes I see are not the same
There is no spark, there is no flame

There is hope, still fighting strong
No matter what, I'll overcome the wrong
From the ones I could trust
I stand in total disgust

I can't let go all thank to you
but understand one day karma is due
And even though my flame is out
I'll bring it back, I have no doubt

Even though I may be cracked
My heart still beats and stays intact

My Heart

My heart is weak
My heart is frail
My heart leads a bleeding trail

My heart is sacred
My heart is true
My heart is not for the likes of you

The way

My heart skips a beat when I lock on your eyes
I wish I knew what you were thinking, where
your intention lies
How I wish to go back and hold your hand
It feels like I'm flying and I don't know where to
land.
The way you smile makes stars collide
I get lost in the moment when I'm by your side
Time stops and everything is mute
You make me warm and feel all cute
This is how you make me feel
Can we let this be real?

I'm Good

I've accepted the emptiness
The feeling of nothingness
The tears are a constant flow
No matter; head high, take it slow
You're here for others and you don't matter
You'll take and take and never shatter
Standing in the room but feels so far away
It's so hard to want to stay
The constant nagging within my mind
Shut if off and release this bind
I want to stop feeling this kind of pain
And silence the voice in my brain
How can someone be so happy
I only feel crappy
I want to wake up and enjoy my day
Instead it's just a constant replay
I hate fighting with myself, and this constant war
I'm tired and don't want to do this anymore
I'm better off alone my mind says to me
But having others is always good, just wait
you'll see
They care and love you
Which I do too
But in the end they have a life of their own
And I'm back stuck in the unknown

What do I do where do I go
Who am I and when will I know
Annoyed, Confused, and over it
The heart is worn and the soul is split
I'm screaming and crying under this hood
But I'll always look up and say I'm good

Survive

It never gets better, that much is true
To cry every night, knowing you have no clue
The walls get closer, the more you breathe
Slowly and slowly, your mind begins to seethe

Smile to pass the day, as you silently go mad
within
Laughing on the outside, screaming underneath
the skin
Not wanting to talk, just let the silence consume
Feeling numb inside, and the wave of gloom

People ask how you are, smile and say I'm fine
Deep down you're sinking, ready to cut the line
Just wanting to let go, to feel anything but the
pain
The voices keep pushing, the darkness will stain

The soul is cracking, the breaking is near
The eyes that stare, you wish no fear
Wipe the tears, can't show the weak
They won't understand, don't give them a peak

Back to "normal", as those would say
Though deep down inside, it's torture to stay

The mind will kill, but the heart beats stronger
To survive again, hold on just a little longer

Therapy

Music is my therapy
It gives me a sense of clarity
It lets me open my seal
To show you how I feel
In a way it's hard to be told
Listen to the lyrics and watch them unfold

Reminded Forever

Behind this smile is sorrow and pain
Tears flowing like endless rain
What you did to me was oh so wrong
My trust is broken and defenses are gone

I can feel the darkness looming over me
And the claws are the only thing I see
I hate myself for leaving you clueless
You left me feeling invisible and useless

Trapped in the deepest part of my mind
Feeling tortured, shackled, and bind
Dark thoughts circle round and round
I'm begging and screaming to be found

The door is shut, temptations rise
The voices start, and begin with lies
Screaming to get them out of my head
Emotions filling full of dread

In the blade I see the faces
The ones that fill the spaces
Gripping my knees and grabbing the throttle
I close my eyes and begin to bottle

My mind is scarred and full of fear
Your mind is happy and all too clear
My life will never be the same
You will be the one to blame

Fight

These tears I shed are full of emotions
These tears I shed are of the commotions

My mind goes on day by day
My mind is confused and full of dismay

Hiding it wont change a thing
Hiding it will come back with a sting

Show them how you feel
Show them you can heal

Never think of picking the knife
Never think of giving your life

Relax

Close your eyes and breathe
Feel the rise of inner piece
Succumb to the calm

Happiness

Happiness is everywhere, sometimes its just
hard to find

Its in the smiles we share with friends
as we gather around Friendsgiving

The laughter we carry with family
Of memories from past to present

It can be the sound of rain as it patters on the
pain
or the rumbling of thunder as it rolls on in

Though you may not see it now, its there just
trust me
Don't live life dull, live life full of joy and
happiness will be there

Mom

She holds me close when I need it most
She rubs my back when I struggle to sleep
No matter the time of day, she'll answer without
delay
She makes me laugh and smile
She shows me how to be brave
Her love of animals is strong and true
No matter what she's always be there
I love you mom, beyond compare

Anxiety

Chest pounding, heart racing
My mind wont stop
Its a constant swap
It gets too much and I begin spacing

I need a moment to think
To breathe and say its okay
You're here don't go astray
Calm and keep in sync

It builds up and falls down
It's hard to focus and keep still
This constant motion I feel ill
I don't want to fall, I don't want to drown

Close my eyes and begin one, two, three
Think of music and hear the tune
It will all be calm real soon
Open now, it's all better you see

Always

I'll always be there
to hold you when needed
to give you a shoulder to cry on
to listen when you need to talk
to bring joy when you're feeling down
I'll always be there for you
because I love you

Finding your why

Write, read, ski
Dance, sing, laugh
Bask in the sun, feel the heat warm your skin
Learn a new hobby
Meet a new friend
Don't watch the time go by
Create new dreams
And live life how you want it to be
Why is the question
Find your Why

Commitment

I'm happy and enjoy life
I'm pissed and want to be left alone
I love the things I do
Even though the stress is too much

I'm dedicated and loyal to those around me,
yet nothing is returned.
Don't worry, you'll see,
the time will come where you need me.

All that's left to say is,
too late

The Shift

Blood boils and temps rise
Mind is overloading no time to comprise

I want to burst and scream
this isn't it, this isn't my dream

I'm not done here you see
though at times I wish to flee

I know I can be strong
It's the matter of how long

I'm Sorry

I'm sorry I couldn't give you more
I'm sorry it's not like before
As time went on we drifted apart
Even deep down, you knew this by heart
We were young and free
Not knowing what's to see
Eye's open now, see the change
Everything's said, you cant re-arrange
I know it's not what you want to hear
It has to be said, it must be clear
I never wish to make you cry
it's time for be to say goodbye

Trust

25

I wish I could have it back
The one thing needed was thrown off track
I struggle now when I see the faces
Of the memories and of those places
The eyes of the strong and true
I never thought it could happen, not even with
you